A Guide To Intuitive Tarot

Facilitate Growth and Healing Through the Power of Tarot

Sarah Vanessa Hayes

COPYRIGHT © 2020, SARAH VANESSA MAYES

Book Title: A GUIDE TO INTUITIVE TAROT
Sub-Title: Facilitate Growth and Healing Through the Power of Tarot
Author: SARAH VANESSA MAYES

ALL RIGHTS RESERVED. Alesia Publishing and its authors recognize all information, including the material in these sacred texts, comes from the collective consciousness. However, no part of this book may be reproduced or transmitted in any form or by any means, electronic or mechanical, including photocopying, recording, or by any information storage and retrieval system wi›thout express written permission by the author. Any unauthorized reprint or use of this material is prohibited.

The intent of the author is only to offer information of a general nature for your general use and well-being. The material contained in this book is for reference only and is not intended to foretell information. In the event that you use any of the information in this book for yourself or others, neither the author nor the publisher assume responsibility for your choices or actions.

Face of the Sun and Moon created by Chikovnaya
Cover Designed by Kristopher Ulley and Pamela Lynch

Author Photography: Kristopher Ulley Photography

Designed and Published by Pamela Lynch, Alesia Publishing

ISBN: 978-1-9990394-2-4

DEDICATION

I have been blessed to have so many believe in me and this Tarot project.

My deepest gratitude is to:

My soul sister and spiritual teacher, Jen Wheaton (Sangat Prakash Kaur)
We met while teaching at the same fitness and yoga studio. Our Aries nature spans both a love of spiritual teachings, our own brand of wacky humour and a fascination with the journey of living. We've enjoyed many road trips to a German-style luxury hotel called Sparkling Hill in Vernon, B.C. renowned for its aromatherapy steam rooms and saunas. We've experienced two Hawaiian islands together and shared the best hike of our lives along the Na-pali Coast. Jen introduced me to the challenging and deeply healing practice of Kundalini Yoga. She embodies the true meaning of teacher and friend, and I aspire to be like her (when I grow up)!

My life and adventure partner, Kris Ulley
We met three years ago and fell in love with such speed and ease! He read my self-published poetry books just to "understand me" better. Kris is my biggest champion and has always waved a flag to celebrate my creative accomplishments with a belief that is completely infectious. We dream about collaborating in a photography and writing project one day.

TABLE OF CONTENTS

DEDICATION		iii
PRAISE		vi
START INSPIRED		ix
1	INTRODUCTION TO TAROT	1
2	MERGING WITH YOUR NEW TAROT DECK!	11
3	MEDITATION, CLEARING AND PREPARATION	19
4	RESPONSIBILITIES OF A CARD READER	27
5	NUMEROLOGY AND TAROT	33
6	HOW TO READ THE TAROT WITH PERSONAL INTERPRETATION	53
7	SYMBOLOGY	63
8	EXPLORING THE MAJOR ARCANA	81
9	CARD SELECTION AND SPREADS	99
10	THE "HOW-TO" STRUCTURE OF A TAROT READING	115
11	THE CARDS IN TAROT SPREAD POSITIONS	125
12	TAROT FOR ANSWERING YOUR CLIENT'S LIFE QUESTIONS	135
WORDS TO UPLIFT YOU!		138
APPENDIX A: COLOUR SYMBOLISM		142
BIBLIOGRAPHY		145
ABOUT THE AUTHOR		147

PRAISE FOR A GUIDE TO INTUITIVE TAROT

"Sarah's book has a great balance of history and knowledge behind Tarot and the cards themselves. She does this while instilling confidence to trust your intuition about what you feel when you're reading for someone. Learning about the cards is only half the story. Practicing and working with the Tarot is just as important, and Sarah's book teaches you both."

— *John McLeod, Toronto, ON*

"I have received many intuitive readings from Sarah over the years. Knowing that she had finally laid out her deep knowledge and wisdom of the Tarot in book form was exciting to me. Sarah has helped me get a much deeper understanding of the energies involved. I also love that she guides the reader to deepen into their intuition, which is something needed for working with this art. This book is a must for those wanting to learn and grow using Tarot."

— *Lyse Collins, Peachland B.C.*

"Sarah helped the Tarot cards come "alive." She enabled me to first get a sense of the cards and then read about what they meant, which strengthened my ability to read them."

— *Tracey Hamilton, Kelowna B.C.*

PRAISE FOR A GUIDE TO INTUITIVE TAROT

"I was completely new to tarot when I took Sarah's course. She taught me how to interpret various aspects of the cards to put together a complete reading. Learning how to use the cards' symbols, colours, numbers, suit and placement was key in helping me build confidence in my readings. "

— *Jenn Young, Vancouver, B.C*

"I have been a regular client of Sarah's for many years and have benefited from her in-depth and deeply intuitive readings. When she said she had a course available in book form, I was super excited. It was just what I needed to gain a better knowledge of the Tarot. Her teachings are clear, easy to grasp and allow the reader to move into a deeper understanding of their intuition."

— *Student*

START INSPIRED

"Our deepest fear is not that we are inadequate. Our deepest fear is that we are powerful beyond measure. It is our light, not our darkness, that most frightens us. We ask ourselves: "Who am I to be brilliant, gorgeous, talented, and fabulous?" Actually, who are you not to be? Your playing small doesn't serve the world. There's nothing enlightened about shrinking so that other people won't feel insecure around you. We are all meant to shine as children do. We were born to make manifest the glory of God (Universe) that is within us. It's not just in some of us; it's in everyone. And as we let our own light shine, we unconsciously give other people permission to do the same. As we're liberated from our own fear, our presence automatically liberates others."

—Marianne Williamson

This quote is the heart of all spiritual work. Honour yourself and also those who are in your presence. Reading cards is an exploration of yourself and humankind. It's a way to study your intuition and your life experiences (both dark, light and everything in between). Also, card reading taps into your innate ability to connect to another person on a soulful level.

Chapter 1

INTRODUCTION TO TAROT

Intentions For the Creation of This Book

- Unravel the mystery around readings and how Tarot cards "work."
- Explore numerology links with Tarot cards.
- Visit traditional card meanings as well as the card's symbols.
- Learn the spiritual responsibility of being an uplifting Tarot reader.
- Curate a variety of different kinds of readings and spread options.
- Build more trust in your own gifts of insight and intuition.
- Learn meditation and clearing options for greater connection in your readings.

- Recognize card patterns to give your readings greater significance.

WHAT IS TAROT READING?

- Cards with symbols and stories revealed.
- A tool to offer insight, hope, direction, and guidance.
- Intuitive coaching, reassurance and relating.
- A spiritual connection means to make interpretations of life's cornucopia of events.
- An understanding and perception of love and life.

WHERE DOES TAROT COME FROM?

Its History

Much of Europe uses Tarot cards to play card games; while in North America Tarot cards are used primarily for divinatory purposes.

Tarot cards can be traced back to ancient Egypt or the Kabbalah, a Jewish oral tradition. There is no documented evidence of the usage of Tarot for premonition purposes before the 18th century. Its origins are thousands of years old.

INTRODUCTION TO TAROT

It's unknown if Tarot is a derivative of the Theosophy System called the Kabbalah or a spiritual doctrine based on mystic translations of the scriptures.

The European version was used starting in the 14th century. The French adaptation was called Tarot, while the Italian version was Tarocci. From the late 18th century until the present time, Tarot has been a road map for mental and spiritual pathways.

Tarot is comprised of two parts: the major and minor arcana.

The major arcana have four suits that correlate to the suits of conventional playing cards. Each of these suits has cards numbering from ace to ten and four face cards for a total of fourteen cards per suit.

The Italians' playing cards still depict the 14th-century symbols today: Wands, Cups, Swords and Pentacles, and is much like North America's Spades, Hearts, Clubs and Diamonds. They relate to the same order as the symbols above.

Tarot's distinguishing feature is a separate 22-card trump suit. It begins with cards that take the reader on the journey of The Fool (Innocence) and ends at The World (Wisdom).

It is believed that the Church of Rome extinguished the use of Tarot cards, as it felt those philosophies were in direct competition with the Church. This led to banning Tarot as a method of divination for two hundred years. The thought was that Tarot might put the power of God into the hands of mere mortals. Fortunately, Tarot survived. It's fascinating to note that the Vatican has the most extensive occult library in the modern world now!

Three of the most popular Tarot decks used today were founded in England in 1888 and originated with members from the group called the Golden Dawn. Its members are credited with the creation and design of The Golden Dawn Deck, the Rider-Waite Deck, and the Thoth Deck.

FIVE STEPS TO SELECTING YOUR TAROT DECK

1. There is a rumour in the Tarot world that your Tarot deck should only be gifted or handed down. It's far better to select a deck that suits and speaks to you.

2. Visit a metaphysical store and touch the sample card decks. Look at the imagery to get a sense of the theme and if they light you up or pique your interest. If you do not have a shop

close by, use the internet to view samples of the cards' imagery as there are hundreds of themes of cards imaginable.

3. If you're new to Tarot, I recommend that you begin with the Hanson Roberts Deck. Its main theme has a Fairy Tale feeling. It's the deck I learned from and it's an approachable starter deck. A popular deck to start learning with is the Radiant Rider-Waite Deck. It's like the perfect little black dress in Tarot form.

   Oracle cards are another divinatory realm and can be a huge departure from traditional Tarot card reading. Oracles, such a cool word, have their own specific companion book that is only applicable to that card deck. Tarot, on the other hand, has archetypes and general themes that can be transferable from deck to deck.

4. Find a card size suitable for your hands that you'll enjoy shuffling. Too small can prove awkward. Too large will have cards falling out and may cramp your hands. Make sure the cards are appealing to your eye and feel good in your hands.

5. Now, get out there and buy your cards. You'll need them as we progress through this book! Feel free to skip buying the large companion book. The small one that comes with it will suffice.

As your knowledge of Tarot grows, and you collect more decks of cards, you'll find the imagery of other decks building layers. It enhances the meaning you give each card in your new decks. As you search for a new deck, choose one that has "Tarot" in the title.

CREATING YOUR OWN TAROT/SPIRITUAL HISTORY "STORY"

The Power of the "Elevator Speech"

An "Elevator Speech" allows you to inspire others with a succinct message, in 30 seconds or less. It's a concise mini-biography that you can recite with confidence to reveal how you are the one to help them.

Let's start with my long-form elevator speech:

My interest in the Tarot began in my early teens. I was thrilled in a way I could not explain when I spent time in a local metaphysical store. It smelled of nag-champa incense, and had shelves stuffed with books on topics like the occult and witchcraft. To my delight it sold crystals, and Tarot and Oracle Card decks.

My first Tarot deck, the Hanson-Roberts unfolded a new world of reading cards. It developed my connection with intuition that extended to other peoples' lives. Its fairy tale depictions provided a stark contrast to my tumultuous teen challenges.

To assist in memorizing the metaphors and symbols represented by each card, I began a Tarot journal.

Through picking a card daily and paying attention to the events of my day, I developed an instinct for each card's association to my life experiences.

By my early twenties, I had cultivated a following of friends and family who utilized my readings as beacons for their life paths and choices. My readings illuminate universal truths for my clients, which helps with clarity of direction and upliftment in dark and confusing times.

As a fitness and yoga studio manager, I moonlight as a "Tarot Reader and Lifepath Coach."

A shorter version sounds something like:

My interest in the Tarot started in my early teens. I

began writing my own Tarot journal, adding to it over the years. By my early twenties, I had cultivated a following of friends and family who utilized my readings as beacons for their life paths and choices. My 'day job' is as a fitness and yoga studio manager, and I moonlight as a Tarot Reader and Lifepath Coach. I offer readings in person, via phone, video or email.

PRE-PLAN YOUR ELEVATOR SPEECH.
You may choose to offer readings professionally, just for fun and practice, or for your own personal guidance. People are generally inquisitive when they hear you study Tarot card reading. It can open up a great way for you to find clients and people who are willing for you to practice this new tool with.

Let's start with your extended version:
It could include your interest in Tarot cards, your spiritual journey, who has inspired you, and what you wish to inspire in others. Don't overthink it. Write from your heart.

_____

_____

_____

INTRODUCTION TO TAROT

Once you have written your extended version, ask yourself what you're willing to share with strangers and friends.

Create your summarized version.

_____

_____

_____

_____

_____

_____

_____

Now when they ask you what you do, you can quickly introduce them to Tarot and invite them to experience a Tarot reading with you.

Chapter 2
MERGING WITH YOUR NEW TAROT DECK!

Once you open your new Tarot deck, there is an imprinting stage in which your physical energy, heart, and intentions blend with your brand new impressionable deck.

There is a merging period that shows respect for the ancient practice of reading cards. Its great power is to heal and transform lives with the help of you as the translator.

Draping your cards in silk, or placing them lovingly in a soft silk bag when they are not in use helps to 'set' the imprint you are seeking to make on the cards. Be mindful to not toss the deck aside or tightly wrap it in an elastic band as that does not honour the cards as an 'alive' entity. Here's how to show reverence to your cards:

- Touch the cards.
- Shuffle them often.
- Admire their beauty.
- Feel the excitement of the newness of them.
- Honour the potential they have to guide and illuminate life paths for so many people.

Your connection to your cards is intangible but powerful.

I highly recommended that in this initial merging phase, you are the only one to touch your cards. It's not to foreshadow something awful occurring if someone curiously picks them up or reaches for them. The idea is for your energy to really meld with the cards before you start readings for yourself and perhaps, eventually others.

The next step is to start doing daily readings for yourself.

Purchase a journal specifically for this purpose. It is tremendously insightful when you revisit daily events and the card you selected that morning or throughout the day.

You may pick up on card patterns that match life patterns and lessons you discover.

You may find the cards illuminate an essential study of yourself. It is valuable to become the 'experiment' or 'guinea pig' to reference cards as they relate to what is occurring in your life. You'll begin to see the connection between real-life events, your daily card selection, and the literal meaning from the accompanying handbook that came with your cards.

Tarot is a lifelong study.

Similar to learning to play the violin or piano, you begin to realize that you learn and progress with every reading. It can feel daunting, overwhelming and even challenging at times! There is such magic to the growth that comes from mastering any craft, especially when you get to share what you learn along the way.

New cards offer a unique perspective and a fresh approach.

I stayed with two decks for the first decade of card reading until I realized my readings had grown stale and lacked innovation. I added a new deck every two to four years to discover new insights and messages. This allows me to create individualized readings and prevents my messages from growing rote or feeling repetitive (for my repeat clients and me).

It is common for a Tarot reader to collect eight to ten decks that they regularly switch between for variety and pleasure. Consequently, clients, friends, and family receive a unique and specialized reading as a particular deck was selected specifically for them.

TRADITIONAL TOUCHSTONES IN TAROT

There's a Minor Arcana and Major Arcana in Tarot.

Minor Arcana in Tarot is anywhere from 40 to 56 cards, which include the original suits of:

- pentacles, coins or disks
- cups
- swords
- wands, rods or batons.

Within each suit, you'll find the cards numbered from ace (or one) through ten.

MERGING WITH YOUR NEW TAROT DECK!

Some decks are similar to a playing deck of cards, and include:

- Pages
- Knights
- Queens
- Kings

The **Major Arcana** traditionally included face cards using roman numerals 0 through XXI (the number 21). Roman numerals were used to depict the numbers on the Major Arcana cards. This part of the Tarot is almost always 22 cards.

Some decks will add in extra cards, such as the Psychic Tarot which has seven chakra cards added to the deck.

Tarot of the Silicon Dawn has 97 cards in total with extra trumps (Major Arcana), extra suit cards (Minor Arcana) and a partial 5th suit called "the Void."

The benefit to start reading Tarot with a more traditional Tarot deck is that it broadens your ability to carry each card's 'original' lessons and imagery to decks that you choose to explore and use in the future. You're learning to read more into the card than expressed in the handbook. As you read, this knowledge adds layers of meaning to each card over time.

Compare the two examples:

1. The OSHO Zen Tarot deck:
   The XVII "Silence" card reveals a night sky with a woman's face silhouetted and in her third eye position is a full moon.

2. The more traditional deck is the XVII "Star" with a depiction of a nymph-like woman pouring water into a pool by starlight.

Remember, both interpretations allow you to expand the meaning of the card.

A side note on reading cards in their "Reversed" position.

The "Reversed" position pertains to reading cards in their upside-down positions if the cards get mixed that way. I felt that it over-complicated my initial understanding of the cards. Now, the reversed position readings feel unnecessary to me as there is such richness to their upright positions!

MERGING WITH YOUR NEW TAROT DECK!

To further complicate matters, the reversed card position is not as simple as the opposite of the upright position. For example, one meaning for the upright Devil card is grappling with our addictions while the reversed doesn't mean the absence of or overcoming addiction.

It's a personal choice, of course, so feel free to explore your readings both ways before choosing to accept or reject the addition of reversed card meanings.

Chapter 3

MEDITATION, CLEARING AND PREPARATION

Before you read for yourself or anyone else, there is a need to settle and root yourself both physically and emotionally. The experience of Tarot readings is much like a surge of energy that can be unpredictable in intensity, duration and effect.

As a spiritually-minded person, your rituals honour the Creator. It opens you to become your client's channel of spiritual knowledge, lessons and information that often transcends the human experience. As a Tarot reader, you become a translator of symbols and metaphors.

A mantra or meditation ritual clears the mind of stress, thoughts, and residues of interaction you had throughout the day. It helps to clear the cobwebs of dreaming if your reading is done in the early morning and is a wonderful path to self-preparation. Your preparation can be a poem, song, piece of scripture or the words of a loved one that you say to yourself. The key is to send a signal to your psyche to welcome in a burst of intuition and love. In essence, the purity brought into you with those chosen words will assist you in preparing your nervous system to embrace the surge of Spiritual energy.

My mantra comes from one of my Spiritual teachers. It helps me to blend my humanness with my Spirit and harness it to my heart before I begin a reading. I often stand when reciting my mantra as I feel rooted to the Earth.

This can be done sitting or standing still with your eyes closed. Repeat silently to yourself and with great love, the following words from Cheryl Forrest:

>I am the Soul.
>I am the Light Divine.
>I am Love.
>I am Will.
>I am Fixed Design.

While silently repeating this mantra to yourself, choose what deck of cards you're drawn to for yourself or the person you are reading for.

MEDITATION, CLEARING AND PREPARATION

- Smudging (See **A STEP BY STEP SPACE CLEARING CEREMONY**)
- Meditation (guided, mantra-based or sitting quietly observing ourselves internally)
- White Light Encasing
- Crystals (Amethyst and Clear Quartz)
- Incense
- Grounding Work
- Prayer
- Deep Breathing
- Releasing Fear
- Cleansing and Rebalancing of Chakras
- Personal Affirmations
- Music or a particular sound or instrument
- Intention setting for the reading, i.e. "I am an ambassador for great love and light when I read the Tarot."
- Yoga (flow of postures or balance pose such as 'Tree' or 'Triangle')
- Essential oil or diffuser, i.e. lavender, eucalyptus.

CLEARING METHODS

List your top three methods to clear and prepare yourself before a Tarot reading:

- ◆ _____
  _____
  _____

- ◆ _____
  _____
  _____

- ◆ _____
  _____
  _____

WHAT IS SPIRITUAL PROTECTION?

Spiritual protection is only needed in the rarest cases.

I have not encountered extreme darkness or evil in my twenty-five plus years of doing readings. Should you encounter this sort of phenomenon, it would be best to consult your Spiritual Teacher or advisor for guidance on how best to proceed.

MEDITATION, CLEARING AND PREPARATION

Your experience may be hallmarked by feeling:

- drained of your energy
- challenged by another person's ego
- or an unexplained sense of fear.

Physically removing yourself from a shared environment may prove to be enough. There may be circumstances where there is a lingering negative vibration in your energy field that does not clear immediately.

Your sensitivity allows you to become a vessel to channel the communications through the cards or messages. Your awareness may become heightened through the reading. It is essential not to ignore or attempt to push away any of your feelings. Honour and acknowledge them as a vital part of your intuition and internal safety system.

Refer to the above list of **Clearing Methods** and experiment with your preferred ways to nurture your sense of well-being. Trust your guidance and know you are protected through the process.

A STEP-BY-STEP SPACE CLEARING CEREMONY

Gather the following items:

- Smudge stick or bundle
- Matches
- Bowl or large shell
- Large feather

Instructions:

PART ONE: Cleanse Yourself

1. Light the end of the smudge stick.
   Let it burn for a couple of minutes until it starts to smoulder.
   Blow on it for the smoke to continue.

2. Call on the Creator to cleanse and protect you and say, "Sacred Sages, please drive away all impurities from my heart centre, and allow them to be removed."

3. Waft the smoke with the feather towards your heart. Take the smudge smoke over your head, arms, and in front of your body while releasing all negative thoughts, feelings and residues.

MEDITATION, CLEARING AND PREPARATION

4. Bring the smoke down your back and towards the ground. Imagine the energy is being returned to the Earth and Air. Imagine you are now fully engulfed in loving, supportive energy.

PART TWO: Cleanse Your Room

1. Call on the Creator to bring in balance and harmony.
   Repeat the sage lighting process.
   Walk around the room you wish to clear and waft smoke into each corner.

2. Move to the centre of the room.

3. Turn east and call on the Creator of Air and say, "Great Creator, please cleanse and inspire this space." While saying this, fan the smudge smoke outwards four times and repeat fanning process in steps 4-8.

4. Turn south and call on the Creator of Water and say, "Please strengthen and bring peace to this space."

5. Turn west and call on the Creator of Fire and say, "Please energize and protect this space."

6. Turn north and call on the Creator of Earth and say, "Please ground and cleanse this space."

7. Look towards the sky, waft smoke four times, and say, "Great Creator, please protect this space from above."

8. Get close to the floor, waft smoke four times, and say, "Great Mother Earth, please nurture this space from below."

9. Put down your smudge tools. Stand and visualize the great Spirits standing on guard for this room. Pay gratitude to them all.

Chapter 4

RESPONSIBILITIES OF A CARD READER

A wise mentor once told me that the mission of a Tarot reader is to assist the recipient to fall in love with themselves. This is my mantra upon preparing for a reading.

This is done in many ways:
- encouraging your client that they are in the exact right place in their life
- reminding them of their gifts of character (as indicated by cards or intuited by you, the reader)
- reminding them of their uniqueness and, therefore, importance in the world
- congratulating them for all they've learnt, overcome and endured as life lessons and challenges.

As empaths, the ability to offer them kindness is extraordinary. May you strive to provide this to your clients. Our human hearts are the gatekeepers of secrets, regrets, soft spots, sensitive causes, loss, grief, mistrust, deep spiritual belief and longings for dreams not yet achieved. The reading allows your client to see themselves through your lens. As you become a mirror for them, you give them permission to celebrate themselves as miraculous.

It is important to remember that the recipient of a reading often comes to you in a vulnerable state. Whether they articulate it or not, they crave kindness and being nurtured. Remember that words can charm, spellbind and comfort.

Many of us have wounds that need healing, and offering love and tenderness to your readings will become instinctual. Clients may come to you unaware they are suffering, and look to you for the wisdom and guidance that they are seeking in their lives.

People are looking for affirmation that the way they are living their life is "right." They seek confirmation that they are travelling along the path most suitable and ideal for them. People refer to it as their fate, destiny, life path, or living up to their potential.

RESPONSIBILITIES OF A CARD READER

It is important to remember that everything is exactly as it should be.

This message of affirmation could be peppered throughout the reading and in conjunction with another encouraging card. A good example of this would be: "I see you are feeling in touch with your intuition (Moon XVIII) and sensing it deepening. What a beautiful affirmation from the Creator that you are on the right path!"

People often equate positive life events, such as happiness, pleasure, and healthy relationships as gauges of whether they are on the right journey. Linking up what you see in the cards with this affirmation of being on track will bring warmth and comfort from the reading that your clients yearn for.

Having faith in yourself as a reader requires practice and a huge dollop of trust in the process.

Sometimes our own beliefs will not mirror or gel with our client's, and that is fine. We do our best to read cards without our biases intruding; however, we are human. One belief that I subscribe to is the theory that nothing is "predestined" or "etched in stone." Therefore, that bias does influence the way I read cards. By seeing certain cards, we gain knowledge about potential life events. This influences us to course correct the path we were on before seeing that card.

That is the nature of readings: ever-fluid, ever-changing and an open interpretation as you glimpse into someone's life.

Much like a photograph, the reading is a snapshot freeze-framed in time. Once the client has chosen you, and you begin to work together, their life direction changes as a result of the snapshot.

For this reason, I dismiss the divinatory expectation that some people have equated with Tarot cards. We cannot predict the future because of free will. It may be prudent to explain this to new clients and deconstruct any expectation that a reading is guaranteed to predict the future.

Resist "fishing" for information at the onset of the reading. Instead, ask a general question such as, "What brings you in for a reading today?"

Certainly, if a client wishes to discuss issues, reasons or key points in their life, then listen compassionately. This interaction must occur at the client's initiation and not yours.

RESPONSIBILITIES OF A CARD READER

A brief explanation of the types of spreads, readings and information is soothing for your client and gives purpose and direction to your time together. Look to your client's eyes for messages about who they are and how they feel, and less to their outer appearance, attitude or demeanour.

Generally, the media and the public still know very little about decoding the sacred mysteries of Tarot cards and readers. One of the images portrayed is the turban-clad, crystal ball caressing, elderly woman who speaks of heartbreak, illness and quite possibly the end of your life. It's no wonder the media has misconstrued the essence of Tarot.

Although the onus does not fall fully to the reader to debunk and demystify the Tarot, a brief explanation of Tarot cards as a symbolic tool of insight can help eradicate the stereotypes. Also, cards such as the Death, Devil, and The Hanged Man are often taken literally instead of figuratively as is the Tarot's true interpretation. If "heavily worded" cards come up in a client's reading, pause to explain that they may represent an opportunity for rebirth or transformation.

Even though Tarot readers may not be professional counsellors or social workers, there is the potential for coaching. To develop trust, remind your client that the reading will be kept confidential. They may feel more inclined to express themselves without censorship. The sacredness of a reading allows them to be seen and understood. Their comfort in being open with you as their reader is imperative to this process. This privacy pledge is especially crucial if the client is a family member, friend or acquaintance. If you're asked details of a particular person's reading, having shared your confidentiality policy serves to strengthen your integrity as a reader.

Even though this wisdom illuminates your client's spiritual work, the very baseline of readings is for their entertainment!

Chapter 5

NUMEROLOGY AND TAROT

Numerology lays a good foundation for any reading.

Numerology in Tarot uses half of the deck known as the Major Arcana. They are trump cards that represent a particular number associated with an influence, energy, archetype and life path.

Typically, I start all my new clients with the following form of Numerology to discover insights about their life themes.

DISCOVERING YOUR PERSONAL YEAR NUMBER

To find your current number:

1. Add your month, day of birth, and the year in which you had your last birthday.

2. Add each digit of that total to get your number.

   Example: April 2, 2019 is
   04 + 02 + 2+ 0+ 1+ 9 = 18.

   If the number you come up with is greater than 21, then add the final numbers together.

   Example: Sept 19, 2019 is:
   09 + 1 + 9 + 2 + 0 + 1 + 9 = 31.

   The number is higher than 21.
   Add 3 + 1 together to equal 4 or 1V.

   This number then corresponds with the card 1V (4) in the Major Arcana representing the theme of **The Emperor**.

   This number changes on your next birthday.

Try It Out!

_____

_____

_____

3. Look up your card.

I The Magician

This year accentuates alchemy and mingling in various ways. The parts of our lives that were once separate benefit from being merged. This conscious combining creates exciting outcomes and adventures for you. You may benefit from blending a new life alchemy; mix the same ingredients you have known in different amounts and a new order.

The Magician card speaks to the importance of gratitude to assist with perspective shifts. You may wish to seek oneness with the self and the Universe through transformative practices such as yoga, meditation, service work, and great journeys to deeply spiritual places.

This card is ruled by creative fires and is an optimal time for you to allow your imaginings to become masterpieces. The Magician card is known as a master communicator.

II The High Priestess

This marks a personal year of independence. You will find you have little tolerance for feeling limited or restricted by the expectations and oppression of other people. This sentiment extends to personal and worldly circumstances.

There is less focus on commitment to relationships and marriage. Your direction now leads you to be on your own to pursue a more purpose-driven and spiritual life. It is the time to connect to your Soul's calling to deepen into your Spirit. Living near water or being magnetized to water is a characteristic of this card. You feel a deep need for balance and harmony. The possibility of withdrawal from disharmonious situations occurs, as your life now orbits a creative cycle.

III The Empress

Strive for more equilibrium and balance in your emotions this year, as The Empress invites you to assess your emotional needs versus wants. It's favourable for you to connect with your true desires in your emotional relationships. Opportunities arise to resolve any lingering issues with maternal figures. Attempt to balance your emotional expression by not over-extending yourself and over-nurturing others. This will bring an innate sense of harmony to your life as you tend to, and re-discover, your true self. Celebrate the clarity you achieve this year.

IV The Emperor

The Emperor is the card of significant change and fresh new beginnings! There will be a focus on becoming a leader or being in a leadership role. It is a magnificent year to start a business! You may find yourself with increased responsibility as a director or manager. It is also a favourable time to start new projects, jobs, and interests. Seek out the wisdom of leaders or influencers in your industry for guidance.

This card has a strong male affiliation, and you'll likely be called to resolve any issues around fatherhood or father figures.

Visual arts and photography have a heightened influence during this time. Travel is featured in a big way this year!

V The Hierophant

The Hierophant represents a year of learning and teaching. It may involve family or people close to you. You may consider going back to school or taking specialized training. When the student is ready, the right teacher emerges.

Past issues or undesired patterns may resurface, which allows you to resolve or handle them differently with your new perspective on life. This is a year of settling into living the life you re-created during your previous year of the Emperor.

There is an emphasis on music and art, which provides healing and nurturing during the year.

VI The Lovers

Previous years have revolved primarily around the inner journey. The year of the Lovers emphasises relationships and provides a forum for growth, inner exploration and learning.

As people are the centre of your year, working with the group mindset is highly favoured. You may confront some major crossroads where you are called to make decisions in your relationships. It is the most common year for traditional relationship milestones. They vary from engagements, marriages, deeper trust and commitments, to separations, divorces and relationships ending.

Your learning comes from all manner of interactions with people. Due to your previous inner work, you may see a shift in your relationships with friends, family and co-workers.

VII The Chariot

You will see an acceleration of the changes and intentions you set in motion three years ago (in the year of the Emperor). This year has a fast pace; it's the "be careful what you wish for" year in a tremendously useful way. Pay attention to what you focus on and intend, as you are in a high manifestation cycle and may easily attract your desires.

You may find yourself adjusting to relationship choices you made last year. Change is the theme here. There is an emphasis on thoughts and planning that influence your family and home, your career and job, frequency of travel or a shift in finances. You may be inspired to redecorate your surroundings or at the very least to rearrange the furniture. There is a feeling of more vitality, positive flow and hustle even when sleep and self-care takes a back seat.

VIII Justice

The scales of justice represent balance and re-balancing. Your finances will come back into balance, especially given the speed of the prior year.

This is a most favoured year to handle legal issues

and settlements. As a result of finalizing things, it's an ideal time to bring forth new ideas and allow them to manifest into physical form. Allow your focus to settle on attempting to balance your health and care of your temple. Remaining grounded in your body, mind and Spirit is crucial to your well-being after last year's busyness and changes. Exercise and yoga will help you achieve emotional and physical balance.

It's a year hallmarked by a resolute desire for life to be simple, direct and clear. There is a feeling of intolerance for anything that remains complex, covert, or non-direct.

IX The Hermit

This year urges the resolution of past issues. The Hermit symbolizes transition and patience with the awakening process. With humility, you can rely on movement in new directions.

Look to your elders for the key to innovative living, creative problem solving and a new perspective. The desire to have life be free and clear of complexity from last year deepens. Be sure that you don't compromise your values and beliefs.

There is a duality of teaching and learning this year with a need to have meaningful and significant experiences. The contrast is that you'd rather spend your time in solitude. It is prime for study, reading, researching and meditation.

This yearning for alone time is due to the need to digest your life's completions with an eye to the horizon to create new beginnings, opportunities and journeys.

X The Wheel of Fortune

All the groundwork laid in years previous come to fruition: healing, introspection, change and your desire for growth.

This is the card of synchronicity and a year of personal breakthroughs. Your connection to your spirit is stronger when you harness the power of the Law of Attraction. Use the feeling of flow to steer your life in more fortunate and positive directions.

There is a great deal of emphasis on self-realization and truth this year.

Unexpected abundance comes in many forms, such as:

- ◆ creative proposals and partnerships
- ◆ money flowing from different, new and unexpected sources

♦ attainment from your past investments of time and energy.

Dreaming and planning become significant because of your ability to manifest powerfully in this particular cycle. It is as if you hold a magic genie lamp.

Enjoy this incredibly fortunate time in your life. Remember, its level of joy mirrors your ability to be honest with yourself about your innermost desires and true spiritual calling.

XI Strength

This is the year to demonstrate your creative and physical strength. Allow your multifaceted self to converge with your talents, aptitudes, skills and interests. Celebrate with a sense of wonder, awe, passion, vitality and excitement! You have earned the right to rejoice for doing the work. It is your badge of honour for having fought for yourself and triumphed.

This is a year where your internal core is empowered and solidified. Look to those in your life who are creative and passionate for guidance and inspiration.

The Strength card is also known as the symbol for the theatre. You are gifted in playing many different roles well, so seek out variety to expand your horizons. Be curious about new and limitless possibilities.

With self-trust, you can develop and rely on your strong spiritual core to live life more focused on the light.

XII The Hanged Man

This is a time in which you feel as if life is hanging in suspension. The energy of The Hanged Man facilitates an opportunity to see recurring issues from a fresh perspective. There is a choice to accept and surrender at this point. It may be a welcome rest or an intensely frustrating time, depending on the work that remains. This is a prime period for an in-depth investigation into unresolved emotions that you haven't fully expressed, such as grief.

If there is fatigue from repeating past patterns, the energy of this card can assist you in breaking the paradigms with a new approach or way of thinking. You develop a consciousness that, at its core, breaks the cycle.

The golden opportunity this year is to resolve and rebalance your karma.

XIII Death

It is a year of intense transformation. This card represents the cocoon aspect of the life cycle in its metamorphosis into a butterfly. The emergence from the cocoon holds many unknowns, and it can be difficult to imagine where you will end up.

This card asks you to have faith and trust in the process. As you become closer to your soul's actuality throughout this year, you are asked to let go to embrace the inevitable.

There is a personal metamorphosis on the horizon, which may include:

- a change in qualities, attributes and interests
- your appearance and style
- your attitude and behaviour
- your belief systems about the world
- the people you choose to have in your life
- your identity.

The death card symbolizes the emergence of a more authentic representation of who you are. Whatever that butterfly looks like, there is an inner beauty in the outcome that's unlike any other human excavation experience.

XIV Temperance

Moderation in all things is the mantra for this year!

It's a time of assimilation, integration, and stabilizing after the shifts experienced last year.

There is also an appreciation and seeking of balance, beauty and harmony. Peaceful surroundings and a relaxed environment at home are needed. You may find yourself actively involved in a significantly creative or passion-fuelled project, group or cause. Lessons may arise surrounding over-consumption, over-doing and over-extension of time, money, and resources. These may linger so that the qualities of Temperance are honoured.

XV The Devil

This year will have a delicious combination of working hard and playing hard. Adopt a willingness in this time to view your own 'bedevilments' or 'shortcomings.' We are asked by life to consistently regard ourselves as projects under construction and never as finished entities. To be finished would diminish our vast potential for limitless growth. There is an exploration of contrast that invites you to look at the various dimensions of yourself. Rather than taking yourself too seriously, this is a good year to welcome in your sense of humour.

This card highlights the experience of strong physical relationships. Facilitate romance and sensuality by being more free-spirited and true to your own desires.

Strong pulls to indulge in the areas of substances (food, alcohol, drugs), screen-time, work, romantic relationships (time together, sex, co-dependence) exist this year. The timing is ripe to analyze your go-to coping mechanisms when life becomes stressful, lonely, overwhelming, or the unexpected happens. Learn to cultivate healthy self-care. It could be a game-changer to interrupt tendencies towards overindulgence.

XVI The Tower

The Tower is a year to rebuild and reinvent yourself, your ideas, residence, lifestyle and health. In essence, it's about extracting the positive energy despite the feeling that life has crumbled down around you.

There has been and may still be a restructuring process of your old life and a focus on restoring what is known at a deep level as truth for yourself. Although you may need to grieve the collapsed foundation you had built your life upon, there is a deep knowing that it was truly for the best. The opportunity to re-create the canvas of your life becomes the focal point. Your choices now will colour the new life you are building. Great healing may be found in creativity, movement and connection to nature. It's visually healing for us to see the beauty of the world through a new lens, such as painting, photography, woodwork, and gardening. An emphasis on health and wellness assists your capacity for reinvention by exploring fitness, dance, yoga and even new recipes!

XVII The Star

The true essence of this card is to enjoy the experience of your enlightenment. There is a sense of awe and inspiration during this year with the culmination of energy that builds self-confidence and self-trust. Last year's destruction and re-building pave the way towards peace and recovery.

This is the most favoured year in the Tarot for external recognition and accolades to celebrate your achievements. You may attract ideology and information to further your spiritual evolution this year.

This heralds the dawning of understanding behind the challenges, grievances and struggles during the past two years. These highs and lows are what give life its colour, melody, and nuances. It's an opportunity to embrace a feeling of lightness in your life.

XVIII The Moon

The moon is about intuition and what remains to be discovered. There are layers of understanding still to be revealed to tap into your many empathic, perceptive and even psychic abilities. As you explore life's many mysteries, your life perspectives will take shape differently.

Light and shadow are predominant themes in this card. Recognize that light and dark co-exist in you to facilitate more self-acceptance. We are all made up of light and dark and everything in between. As a result, you become able to access more profound levels of honesty this year. This provides clarity in the knowledge of what choices need to be made in the areas of love, family and career. Consulting with your inner guidance before making these choices is your greatest ally at this juncture.

XIX The Sun

You and your life are inspired in the phase of The Sun. The Sun brings joy, harmony and happiness in the Tarot. New opportunities to follow your heart may result in leaving teams or projects behind. Pursue your dreams with as few distractions as possible this year.

This is the best year to collaborate and begin creative projects. There's a desire to experience a sense of community and cooperation. A sense of well-being fosters growth and togetherness with friends.

There is a huge love component to this year as the sun is affiliated with warmth and light. Friendship and time with children are highlighted. Continued exploration of perspective allows for more profound compassion and connection to the human collective.

XX Judgement

The Judgement year delves into the layers of self; the process of unpeeling these layers are like removing each ring of an onion to access your different inner voices. There is the inner child's playful and spirited voice, the higher "God-like" self, the knowledge-based and wise self, and the feeling and sensory self. Judgement is a time to connect to all the onion layers for varying expressions of the inner voice. Their blend produces ideas and intuition for your best life outcomes and decision-making efficacy.

You may long to soar bird-like over your life and world in order to take in the bigger picture. Your world has undergone many shifts, particularly in the past five years. Loving with compassion is at the heart of how you respond to what you experience now. You've developed flexibility in your thoughts and creative problem solving, which can be pursued even further. This is a time of integrating with your past to remain perceptive about your present and future.

XXI The Universe

Celebrate your accomplishments and learnings! It's a time of new directions as a result. There is a feeling of completion and enjoyment in being on top of your game. You are inspired to expand and broaden your experiences.

You may discover yourself in a futuristic vision with a deep emotional commitment. Your passion for the world sees you expanding to a new global awareness that may involve emphasis on environmental sustainability and becoming service (volunteer) focused. There is a strong pull to travel: to explore, experience, and enrich your life and those around you. Research is your greatest ally this year as you seek out information on how to delve into entirely new avenues and adventures. This card represents the end of an era for you.

DISCOVERING YOUR RULING NUMBER

Another form of Numerology is to add your day + month of birth to the year you were born to get the theme that will follow you for the duration of your life.

Example:

My birthdate is April 2, 1978.
It's calculated as: 04 + 02 + 1 + 9 + 7 + 8 = 31.

The number must be re-added as it's greater than 21. We then add 3 + 1 = 4.

My Lifetime Numerology card is 1V (4) Emperor, which is about Leadership.

Numerology is a great "appetizer" to any reading and is just as delicious on its own!

Chapter 6

HOW TO READ THE TAROT WITH PERSONAL INTERPRETATION

Explore!

Flip and shuffle your deck. Choose eight cards to work with that "speak" to or inspire you. Write down the card's name and its dominant and prominent colours.

Card #1: _____
Colour: _____
_____
Colour: _____
_____
Colour: _____
_____
Colour: _____
_____

Card #2: _____
Colour: _____
_____
Colour: _____
_____
Colour: _____
_____
Colour: _____
_____

Card #3: _____
Colour: _____
_____
Colour: _____
_____
Colour: _____
_____
Colour: _____
_____

More notes:

HOW TO READ THE TAROT

Card #4: _____
Colour: _____
_____

Colour: _____
_____

Colour: _____
_____

Colour: _____
_____

Card #5: _____
Colour: _____
_____

Colour: _____
_____

Colour: _____
_____

Colour: _____
_____

Card #6: _____
Colour: _____
_____
Colour: _____
_____
Colour: _____
_____
Colour: _____
_____

Card #7: _____
Colour: _____
_____
Colour: _____
_____
Colour: _____
_____
Colour: _____
_____

More notes:

Card #8: _____
Colour: _____
_____
Colour: _____
_____
Colour: _____
_____
Colour: _____
_____

There are traditional meanings given to each card in the Tarot. Many clients appreciate and see value in knowing the true energy of the traditional Tarot as another layer to their reading.

In the beginning, you may be drawn to read the accompanying books and memorize their meanings. This process can take many years to master.

If you want to intuit your decks sooner than that, look to the symbolism in the cards. Using the metaphor and symbols, you can see on each card face is a way to access a reading without knowing the backstory to each card.

A pupil of the Tarot willing to put time into studying the traditional meanings of the cards will find much more to explore and delve into during readings. Researching the accompanying books and traditional archetypes serves to add another layer of meaning and complexity to your readings. We will explore this concept more in the coming chapters.

Let's delve a bit deeper into the eight cards you pulled. This aspect of Tarot is like art: it is highly subjective. It's based on a set of your own personal chosen symbols and story. You decide what the symbols represent:

- the particular hue of the colour red
- a specific version of a star
- the figure of a dark male riding a steed.

It is these subjective interpretations that will allow us to read our Tarot decks with ease!

First, let's brainstorm more on colour.

COLOUR SYMBOLISM: AN EXPERIMENT

Step 1: After reading each colour on the following pages, close your eyes and imagine what the colour represents to you. Create a list of characteristics. You'll then be invited to choose what feeling, meaning or energy is evoked in Step 2.

HOW TO READ THE TAROT

Pink: _____

_____

_____

_____

Red: _____

_____

_____

_____

Orange: _____

_____

_____

_____

Yellow: _____

_____

_____

_____

Green:_____

_____

_____

_____

Blue: _____

_____

_____

_____

Purple: _____
_____
_____
_____

Brown: _____
_____
_____
_____

Black: _____
_____
_____
_____

Grey: _____
_____
_____
_____

White: _____
_____
_____
_____

Step 2: Refer to your list of eight cards.

Look at one card and notice one dominant colour.

Write down what you feel the meaning of the colour is from your interpretation above. For example, red could mean passion, or perhaps frustration, while blue may represent serenity or melancholy.

The imagery on the face of the card gives you context to choose the energy of any colour.

This is an exercise of trusting yourself.

There truly is no wrong answer because, like art, we all see something a little different.

Colour can establish recurring themes in a reading easily. It is a wonderful universal language that the beginning and master Tarot reader alike can rely upon.

Colour is a great tool to incorporate during a reading. For example, I may say to a client, "There are many cards here with green and blue shading. This signifies to me that you are in a time of emotional connectedness and willingness to grow."

The general tone of the card comes to you by practicing and tapping into your intuition. Intuition is a primal instinct, a knowing or tingling feeling of insight. Everyone has it. This exercise may have helped you to reveal your intuition's accessibility.

In summary:

A Tarot card + its prominent colours + your interpretation = your ability to "read" the card.

This is how a reading begins to be built. It's a good moment to pause in triumph and absorb what you've accomplished.

Chapter 7
SYMBOLOGY

Allow your curiosity to be your teacher.

Be guided by the aspects that most appeal to you through the story that the card is revealing.

These are the building blocks to build trust in your intuition. Your ability to connect with the cards is a valuable asset in your journey as a Card Reader!

The depth you crave in Tarot may be well served through researching the many symbols represented by the deck you chose. For instance, a deck with a prominent cultural theme invites us to research that culture to gain a deeper understanding for our clients. Another example would be whether your deck is from the Faerie realm or Fairy tales.

Every single thing on the face of the Tarot card has value and significance. Although the whole breakdown of the card doesn't need to be shared in its entirety, our understanding of the energies of the card are vastly increased as we explore each symbol on the card.

ASTROLOGY AND THE ELEMENTS

Astrology plays a large part in many Tarot decks as the elements are closely associated with the suits in the Tarot.

Cups = Water
Rods =Fire
Disks = Earth
Swords = Air

The Western version of Astrology is usually represented by its animal, a tool used for characterization of people, relationships and health areas.

ARIES (born March 21-April 19)

Sign: FIRE
Symbol: the RAM
Key Phrase: "I am"
Health Area: Head

These are the pioneers of the zodiac and are skilled self-starters. The sign is youthful, impulse-driven and brave. They may experience difficulty completing or finishing projects. The Ram is agile, confident and courageous. They are fond of physical and social activity. Aries are sharp in intellect and tongue.

Other notable traits:
- imaginative
- quick-tempered
- explorers

TAURUS (born April 20-May 21)

Sign: EARTH
Symbol: the BULL
Key Phrase: "I have"
Health Area: Neck and throat

The Bull is known for their gorgeous voices and sensuality! The sign is fond of the good things in life. They revere and appreciate beauty. The Bull is slow to anger but may erupt when pushed too far. They are intentional in their ways and able to see tasks through to completion.

Other notable traits:
- domestic
- patient
- self-indulgent
- artistic
- proud

GEMINI (born May 21-June 21)

Sign: AIR
Symbol: the TWINS
Key Phrase: "I think"
Health Area: Arms and lungs

Geminis are well known for their "dual natured-ness." This trait allows them the insight to see both sides of situations. The Twins enjoys travel, trade and the literary arts.

Other notable traits:
- eloquent
- inventive
- unsympathetic
- adaptable
- curious

CANCER (June 21-July 22)

Sign: WATER
Symbol: the CRAB
Key Phrase: "I feel"
Health Area: Lymphatic system including breasts and stomach

Best known for their attachment to home. They are nurturing parents (although can still be quite attached to their own parents), and are sensitive individuals with a leaning towards moods and a need for security. Sometimes food issues are present.

Other notable traits:
- ◆ kind-hearted
- ◆ intuitive
- ◆ brooding
- ◆ cautious
- ◆ romantic

LEO (July 23-Aug 22)

Sign: FIRE
Symbol: the LION
Key Phrase: "I will"
Health Area: Heart and spine

The Lion is known for its bravery and nobility association. They have a desire to give everything for love. The Leo's ego may be overdeveloped and need praise. They are fond of physical activity and social gatherings, and often crave the spotlight.

Other notable traits:
- affectionate
- ambitious
- domineering
- bold
- loyal

VIRGO (Aug 23-Sept 22)

Sign: EARTH
Symbol: the YOUNG WOMAN
Key Phrase: "I analyze"
Health Area: Intestines, pancreas and hands.

Virgos are hard-working, often exhibit an aptitude to being entrepreneurs and have a knack for accumulating wealth. They make excellent teachers, doctors and nurses, as they live to serve humanity selflessly.

Other notable traits:
- witty
- introspective
- scheming
- fussy
- studious

LIBRA (Sept 23-Oct 22)

Sign: AIR
Symbol: the SCALES
Key Phrase: "I balance"
Health Area: Kidneys and ovaries in women

Libras enjoy company and find themselves through relations with others. Sticklers for fairness, they may become easily upset by social injustices. They are content to let circumstances make choices for them.

Other notable traits:
- intriguing
- suave
- secretive in matters of the heart
- enthusiastic
- imitative

SCORPIO (Oct 23-Nov 21)

Sign: WATER
Symbol: the SCORPION
Key Phrase: "I desire"
Health Area: Nose, bladder, sex organs, adenoids (tonsils) and bowels.

Even though this sign is affiliated with the scorpion, it also has the traits of the snake and eagle. There is a possibility for this sign to go very dark, very light or vacillate between both polarities. The dark sides of debauchery, jealousy, violence and treachery are present in an unbalanced Scorpio. Balanced, they can be powerful healers and social reformers, exuding the highest qualities of humankind. Passion drives them and can be channelled into more than just a physical expression of that sentiment.

Other notable traits:
- altruistic
- imaginative
- quick-tempered
- suspicious
- penetrating

SAGITTARIUS (Nov 22-Dec 21)

Sign: FIRE
Symbol: the CENTAUR/ARCHER
Key Phrase: "I see"
Health Area: Hips, thighs and muscles.

The Sag loves to strive and enjoys physical and social activity. They can be wild and seek adventure and freedom from all restraints. The Archer is a humourous, positive person with a love of entertaining. They value wisdom and are well suited to teaching.

Other notable traits:
- speculative
- jovial
- philosophic
- impatient
- proud

CAPRICORN (Dec 22-Jan 20)

Sign: EARTH
Symbol: the GOAT
Key Phrase: "I use"
Health Area: Joints, skin, gall bladder and teeth.

The goat has a natural association with wealth through hard work. They are planners and strategizers who possess great patience. Capricorns are reserved personality types who may view pleasure-seeking as a waste of time. They are loyal with a hidden sensitive side beneath that exterior of reservation.

Other notable traits:
- economical
- mind-driven
- powerful
- inhibited
- thrifty

AQUARIUS (Jan 20-Feb 18)

Sign: AIR
Symbol: the WATER BEARER
Key Phrase: "I know"
Health Area: Retinas, calves, ankles, body electricity.

Sometimes the Water Bearer is eccentric. They love to work with other people. They have an aptitude for writing and humanistic endeavours and may avoid emotionality by intellectualizing it.

Other notable traits:
- vivacious
- kind
- worrying
- inventive
- well-liked

PISCES (Feb 19-Mar 20)

Sign: WATER
Symbol: the TWO FISH
Key Phrase: "I believe"
Health Area: Feet, toes, lymph and sweat glands.

Sometimes people with this personality are most comfortable in more subtle dimensions than the realms of everyday. They cope with life through art, music, mysticism and sometimes addiction. They have highly developed intuition and psychic qualities. They are loving and compassionate, with an innate sense of emotional security. Otherwise, they may risk becoming obsessed with themselves.

Other notable traits:
- versatile
- loquacious
- introspective
- melancholy
- devoted

SHAPES

Below is a summary of the more common aspects of another layer in readings. More symbols exist than listed below, but these shapes can present an overall theme in the reading. This is especially true if you see them in multiple cards.

Circles: Completion, Perspective, Insight, Joy

Squares: Conformity, Inclusion, Security, Fate

Diamonds: Wisdom, Wealth, Understanding, Promise

Stars: Enlightenment, Hope, Destiny, Laws of Attraction, Miracles

Crosses: The Axis of the World, The Union of Opposites, A Life at a Crossroad

Triangles: A trifecta, building a strong base, otherworldly strength, unearthing your untapped potential, intuition, spiritual gifts.

EXPLORING SUITS & NUMBERS IN THE TAROT

Minor Arcana Suits, Elements and Astrological Associations:

Cups (Water: Cancer, Scorpio, Pisces)
The emotional realm, family, meaningful relationships, what we hold in our hearts.

Rods/Wands (Fire: Aries, Leo, Sagittarius)
The creative force within, abilities, talents, aptitudes and gifts of character.

Swords (Air: Gemini, Libra, Aquarius)
Conflict and resolutions within the self and relationships, willpower, grit.

Pentacles/Disks/Coins (Earth: Taurus, Virgo, Capricorn)
Money, finances, material matters, job, career, business, prosperity and abundance.

GENERAL INTERPRETATIONS FOR MINOR ARCANA NUMBERS AND ROYALTY CARDS:

Aces: Deal with new beginnings and initiating new projects and relationships; raw energy; fresh starts.

Twos: Deal with relationships, duality and balance (re-balancing).

Threes: Represent synthesis, expression, transformative experiences and understanding.

Fours: Represent foundation, stability, status quo and seizing opportunities.

Fives: Deal with change and instability.

Sixes: Represent assistance, idealism and ideas of perfection.

Sevens: Represent unexpected changes (both favourable and unfavourable), perception and insight.

Eights: Deal with control, power over oneself and organizations.

Nines: Represent the highs and lows felt in every life, fulfillment or lack thereof.

Tens: Represent renewal and completion; mastering life lessons.

Pages: Represent either a message coming, or a young male or female under the age of 25.

Knights: Represents men between the ages of 25 and 40 years.

Queens: Represents women over the age of 25 years.

Kings: Represents men over the age of 40 years.

Chapter 8

EXPLORING THE MAJOR ARCANA

The Major Arcana, in its traditional form, is said to be the "Journey of the Fool." This courageous "every man or every woman" has a whole host of challenges and triumphs to undertake as a human being having a spiritual experience in this life. Your deck will have a similar journey or at least a basis of this concept if it's called a Tarot Deck.

Here are my insights into these cards:

0 The Fool

Represents both the beginning and culmination of the experiences each person encounters in the quest for awareness in life. You are exuberant in your willingness to take chances and do not linger long in any one experience. You choose to remain aloof from seductive societal games and may back away from situations involving depth and intensity just as an innocent child might. There is self-reliance in instincts and intuition for protection and guidance. This card heralds a readiness for new adventure and curiosity in life. Opening the mind to a more playful attitude both at work and in recreation, friendship, and love is highly favoured. It is the card of the courageous explorer of life and the world.

I The Magician

You can access a variety of creative resources, and many benefits in focusing on the manifestation of dreams, aspirations, and goals in this state. You have the power to be original, independent and strong-willed; a true master of your Universe. Reality is created by your thoughts, and the awareness of this holds great potential.

The study of metaphysics depicted by this card shows us that harnessing unseen forces to manifest positive situations and people is just the tip of the iceberg with the Magician card. You are ready to trust your resourcefulness and focused will. In the face of stumbling blocks in life, magic reveals itself through intuition and synchronous events.

II The High Priestess

She is a card of spiritual depth and mystery. She speaks only after going deep within herself for great insight. This can be misunderstood as a flaw and viewed as being secretive and unreadable. She can tap into psychic, intuitive, clairvoyant levels and easily reads people's hearts and motivations. Sometimes she truly knows others better than they could ever know themselves as she sees them at their soul level.

Often this woman is a counsellor, spiritual teacher and may do readings for others. Only those who desire depth find her eager to share her gifts of wisdom and spiritual connection. She is known as the one who brings us the messages from the heart of the Universal Consciousness. Her wisdom, once recognized, becomes so valuable and sought after by her deep affection for community.

III The Empress

The Empress symbolizes Mother Nature in all her abundance and ripeness. This is a time of mastery at fostering growth in the physical and material world. This is accomplished by conception and birth, as well as nurturing those in need and who are vulnerable. This card also heralds material prosperity. She's the flower of femininity, values home and family, and appreciates comfort and a peaceful enjoyment of life.

This matriarch often takes an interest in culture and volunteer work for under-privileged and segregated groups in society. Watch for the Three of Cups in the spread to herald pregnancy when coupled with the Empress. She represents a loving energy that is motherly and feminine in a caretaking and friendly way.

IV The Emperor

The Emperor is as patriarchal a card as the Empress is matriarchal. He rules the principles of logic, system, order and the left-brained domain of life, and symbolizes authority figures of all kinds: fathers, executives, law enforcement, leaders, and politicians. His role is one of ensuring order and rules in everyday life. He often is relatable by looking at the way we have perceived the role of our own fathers in our lives, whether encouraging or judgemental, supportive or critical, loving or cold—certainly, a blend of many traits. If one has been rebellious in the past, there may be an opportunity to resolve any overreaction to rules and rule-makers when we see this card. With conscious awareness and thought, old patterns with authority need not be repeated.

Similarly, if you have felt intimidation by authority figures in the past, the chance to bear witness and then release your anxiety about the individuals may present itself. This card has a strength that is solid and firm, the gradations of which are finite and based on your own past experience with the patriarchy.

V The Hierophant

This card was once thought to represent organized religion and its roots in medieval Europe. It was believed that God's law must be interpreted and shared with the masses. In contemporary times, this card reflects the softer and more personal experience of God and the Universe. Many have moved away from the rigid adherence to outside rules in favour of individual moral standards and a blending of spiritual belief systems. Meditation and self-awareness more accurately express the card's energy now. To question and to grow spiritually is in all of us. The call may be louder based on the individual's journey and to deepen a connection to the Spirit within, others and in the Cosmos. Research and exploration of books, religions, yoga practices, meditation techniques, strong spiritual teachers: all assist in replying to the call.

VI The Lovers

This is the experience of falling in love with yourself through a relationship with another. It is the highest card of love in the Tarot deck and goes to a deeper experience of love as it transcends lust and physical attraction. This card can symbolize intense, passionate, and karmic attractions. It works both angles of the "opposites attract" and "like attracts like" philosophies of love. You are simultaneously challenged to learn and grow as individuals and enjoy and relax into the comforts of the relationship. This card can also speak of a difficult choice to be made (not necessarily in matters of the heart) between two appealing paths or alternatives. With self-awareness and reflection, the right decision comes when you consult the heart.

VII The Chariot

The Chariot is the movement card of the Major Arcana. It represents focus and energy on a goal or intention and how that concentration attracts its completion. It's a card of action, motion, and purpose. It reveals that all parts of an individual are engaged (physical, emotional, mental and spiritual) and harnessed as servants of their will.

The Chariot is a high-functioning card and belongs to a person who possesses high self-sufficiency and drive. Often a trip (mostly by vehicle) is indicated. You will proceed full speed ahead toward any achievements and goals where there is a strong call to pursue. The Universe is primed to provide.

VIII Strength

The qualities of the eighth card are gentleness, healing and inner strength. It represents the ability to cope with conflict or crisis with calm confidence and trust that all will eventually be well. It can bring harmony out of conflict and strife. Often this card is associated with good health and those who have the gift of healing others. This person has earned their inner state by enduring many of life's tumultuous situations. You do not overstate your strength but instead hold it near and dear. Strength provides comfort during storms and when you know there is a light at the end of the tunnel. This card can be a reminder that honey is a better attractant than vinegar. The Strength card indicates a time for ease and kindness versus terseness and demands.

IX The Hermit

The Hermit represents a period of contemplation and meditation needed to digest and assimilate external input. The tendency here is to turn inwards to draw strength from your own inner awareness and insights. This card can represent the teacher and the student who values studies and knowledge. Schooling is another avenue represented by this serious card and enrolment is quite often associated with it. Its heart is the quest for self-discovery through inner reflection. It is a favourable time to take classes or seek out a teacher for assistance with life direction. Meditation and inspirational literature help to deepen and highlight your insights at this time.

X Wheel of Fortune

This card's connection is with luck, fate and destiny. Timing is often more important than pure luck, as events have a synchronicity to them. These meaningful coincidences are the Universe's answer to an individual's strong understanding of their desires, which are in alignment with the greatest good for others. If you pay attention and act on your intuitive understanding of these energies, unexpected lucky events come to pass. They move your life into new directions and flow. The ability to adapt to change will determine whether you accept the good luck that the Universe has in spades. There is a titillating feeling at this point in life, a delightful anticipation that something fortunate is about to happen. It is precisely this belief that brings your heart's longings to you.

XI Justice

This is the card of the scales and balance in life. Legal and karmic justices are two aspects of this card. Sometimes karmic justice is challenging to recognize, particularly if the situation was in a past life. This card brings with it balanced judgement and appropriate resolution of inequities. There is a leaning of the scales in your favour here. The lesson of giving more to receive more is part of the karma in this card. Fairness must be the focus of your dealings. When you lose your sense of proportion, even in a good personality trait or interest, the balance becomes off-kilter and needs re-focus. Having moderation and a meditation practice help you to attain a sense of balance.

XII The Hanged Man

This is the crossroads stage of the journey when you must question the more profound meaning and purpose of life. It's a period of polarization, suspended animation and self-sacrifice. To endure this lack of direction means a path to awareness is carved out. Often, it feels like life is "on hold" or has lost direction, and may be a stage of "in-between" jobs, relationships, philosophies, towns. An enforced waiting period is necessary to see past any confusion and understand your real priorities and desires in your journey.

The Hanged Man asks you to trust that this stage is only temporary and will lead you to the next step in your evolution.

XIII Death

This is a symbol of a change of form. The card signifies endings and new beginnings, in the same manner that Winter must return the earth to a dormant state before Spring may bloom. It is a period of profound transformation; you die to a part of yourself that is decaying and is now useless to you. You grieve the ending and are sometimes in denial until a new possibility emerges on the horizon. The caterpillar to cocoon to the butterfly analogy is a perfectly apt metaphor for this card. You must create an incubation time for yourself to change form and become a more mature version of yourself.

The beauty of "seeing" the Death card allows you to remove some of the confusion and grief it may bring. If you can cooperate with the card's energy and allow the stale parts of yourself to be released, space can be created for the new changes within to be revealed. The empty feeling of the in-between stage of this card calls you to walk with a blind trust through this time of transformation. Only the Creator can provide comfort as you are becoming a more authentic and truthful representation of your soul.

XIV Temperance

The alchemy of this card blends the element fire (inspiration and spirit) with water (emotion and intuition). This represents the innate, intuitive sense of timing and proportion that constitutes perfect temperance. You are advised to understand the hidden energies behind timing and moderation. Life flows much more effortlessly with this knowledge, and as you remember that moderation is key to eating, drinking, dieting, and spending. Attuning to the changes in the proper proportion of these areas can change daily and even hourly for us. Clear the channels of mental clutter and work to live life from more than a purely one-sided approach. When you do, temperance and grace come to you to support your goals to mine balance and harmony for your life.

XV The Devil

Each person or their partner is a unique unveiling of their own particular character flaw(s) and addictive behaviour(s). Often, it is what you are most attracted to doing, like a moth to a flame, that burns and singes you seemingly without your ability to pull away from it. This card represents a distortion that is impeding to the self. "Habits" often fall into this mindless category. Cleanliness to the extreme distorts to obsessive compulsive disorder, social drinking to alcoholism, shopping to materialism, affection to stalking, and so on. This card provides a warning of excess. It is the seductiveness of these flaws or behaviours that is the cue to their "be-devilment." You know intuitively that it is a mistake, but the attraction to the weakness is potent. It's quite common that it has taken on a voice of its own that controls your ability to resist it due to its persuasive and manipulative inner dialogue. This card emerges to remind you that a significant step in your growth and understanding lies in dealing with these parts of yourself.

XVI The Tower

The Tower represents a loss of your foundation, both figuratively and literally, and indicates that your plans have not gone as expected. As your sense of security crumbles, you are forced to rebuild your life from the rubble of chaos. This challenging life experience is a necessary human experience to excavate lessons about yourself, your support system and the world around you. This climax of your current storyline is often seen as the "Great Turnaround." As a result, you inevitably create a sturdier foundation based on experience and realism.

The extremes of this card can go to great lengths, such as accidents, bankruptcy, fire, divorce, physical/mental collapse, nervous breakdown or illness. These are lessons about limitations. There is a feeling of being tested by circumstances beyond our control. Letting go helps you to regain some control at this time.

This card represents the metaphor of the phoenix rising in splendour from the ash of a burnt down life. Perhaps you were even the one who lit the match.

XVII The Star

The Star is a card of enlightenment! You must draw upon both the unconscious and conscious levels of yourself to fully grow and express yourself. The Star card inspires us to reach for our highest potential and touch its brightness. Your wishes and dreams help you to actualize your life purpose. A life that is stalwart and lacks meaning pleads with you to attune to your Higher Self for further nourishment and direction. From this attunement, you receive prompts from the Universe to realign with a higher purpose.

It can be an intensely creative card. You imagine your best life and align with what really inspires you, whether its art, music, nature, being of servitude, communing with animals and children, etc. The Star represents a natural alliance to good health, well-being and profound optimism. Fortunately, like attracts like. This flow of positivity is likely to grow exponentially, giving you glimpses of your sense of purpose. With a solid affirmation of your intention, you can be carried on its wings.

XVIII The Moon

This card focuses on the dualities that are inherent forces in the world and yourself. Light and dark complement each other through understanding contrast and anticipation.

The "light" phase of the moon shares characteristics with both The Star and The Sun cards. The light means different things to different people: for some its joy, enlightenment, connection to their gift, or being in service to others.

This card has a massive component of tapping into your unconscious mind and psychic abilities, which is vast in terms of possibilities. It affirms our aptitude to:

- access our intuition by receiving accurate hunches
- see things in the mind's eye before they happen (clairvoyance)
- sense others' emotions or situations (clairsentience)
- feel warmth and electricity in the hands when they are placed on another (healing).

The "dark" phase of the moon represented in this card symbolizes the things that continue to haunt us: secrets, buried memories, paranoia and compulsions. If you continually run away from integrating what you perceive to be your shadow side, then the haunting grows ever more pursuant. With acceptance, you can acknowledge this is a part of the necessary duality that exists in each of us. We all have facets of ourselves that are stifling; nonetheless, we need self-compassion.

Without integration, the splice can create disturbances in the brain and emotions. Mood swings, mental and emotional instability, a feeling of being an outsider are all symptomatic of this. Situations will be presented to allow us to focus on the blend that is ideal for you. Every part of you deserves to be acknowledged, embraced and integrated for true harmony.

XIX The Sun

This card conveys the satisfaction and sheer joy of being alive! It has a child-like quality in its exuberance for the simple pleasures of life. You are fully present in the moment. On an inner level, it refers to creative self-expression without censorship. There is a connection to your Higher Self to experience freedom and expand into all caveats of life.

You are seen as a source of light, upliftment, and radiant warmth.

On an outer level, the card refers to honour, recognition, success and fulfillment of goals. The awareness of the wonderment of life and its many blessings is evident.

XX Judgement

Judgment is a depiction of a joyful resurrection in which the personality unites with the Higher self or soul. It symbolizes the integration of your acceptance of the soul into everyday awareness. This refers to your whole inner person, not merely the identity and thoughts. This is a journey to your centre for peace and elation. You awaken from the illusion that happiness lies outside of yourself. Your spirit finds rebalancing and digests valuable life lessons. The opportunity for more journeying and knowledge is right around the corner.

XXI The World

This card shows the ability to rise to wisdom and knowledge. At this point, you shed some of your worldly attachments in favour of a spiritual journey. You are transcending beyond the physical and mental constructs towards trusting the inner voice, Universe and Cosmos. There is a meaningful understanding about the purpose and role that your life experiences have held for you. They were necessary assistants to your inner development.

Like The Fool card, The World has a gravitational pull towards travel with a desire to see diverse cultures, monuments and to satisfy curiosities about specific places that you've been called to.

This card is the synthesis and culmination of the life adventure. With this chapter complete, a new seed is planted to reveal the next exciting and courageous leap where you get the opportunity to get messy in the business of living all over again.

The World card invites you to celebrate with confidence, the wisdom you have gained through your choices. As you sit in the seat of your new understanding, there is a natural inclination to shine a light on the cobblestones that are yet to come.

Chapter 9

CARD SELECTION AND SPREADS

Shuffling Your Cards!

There are many different ways to shuffle:

- ◆ Shuffle the cards as you would a deck of playing cards.

- ◆ Ask your client to shuffle until they feel done.

- ◆ Spread the cards out on the table in a pile or shape of your choice and have your client select cards equivalent to the spread number you've chosen to read.

- ◆ Make an arc or line and ask the client to visualize that the Tarot shape is a representation of their body. Have them draw cards in relation to where they feel different cards in their body.

For example, tell them the first card in your spread represents the Present. Ask, "Where do you have the first instinct or awareness in your body for the first card position?" Wait for their response.

Then, instruct them, "Now choose the card as if the Tarot deck laying in front of you was your body. The head is at one end, the torso is mid-deck, and the feet are at the other end of the deck."

- ◆ Create a master pile and ask your client to cut the deck into various piles. (You read the top card of each pile.) This option is excellent for 1, 2 and 3 card spreads, but it is not a great option past five piles of cards.

- ◆ Create your own favourite new and improved way.

CARD SELECTION AND SPREADS

Definition of a spread is a grouping of card placements often in a shape. Well-known card spreads are:

- 12 cards: Celtic Cross
  (a general theme of your life)

- 10 cards: Fool's Lifepath
  (where you are in your journey)

- 7 cards: Lover's Paths
  (how you relate to one another)

- 5 cards: Distant past, past, present, future, distant future

- 3 cards: Past, present, future

There are thousands of spreads that can be used, and we will explore more options later in the book.

Add Awareness and Accuracy:

- Keep the cards face down until you are ready to place cards in their respective positions on the table in their spread. This is the fun part—the moment when you turn all the cards over for The Reveal!

- Ask your client to choose their cards with their left hand. There's a deep connection between the left hand and right brain. Our right brain is known for its heightened creativity. It's the gate through which we can enter into parts of our unconscious mind; the part of ourselves often referred to as the Divine within.

- Encourage first impulses. If cards fall out while you or the client are shuffling, read them as a message "here and now" for the client. Overthinking or trying to feel heat or energy from cards does not usually provide as much accuracy as first instincts.

- Choose cards from your "gut" (feeling self) instead of through the eyes. Closing the eyes while choosing can assist with this.

- Trust yourself to choose cards. Resist any

inertia. Each reading is an ever-changing fingerprint of life, and there is no wrong interpretation. Tarot is merely one perspective.

A small side note: *Valuable time can be lost if the shuffling and choosing cards method is too complex. It is merely the entranceway to the castle; do not linger too long at the gate.*

CHOOSING A SPREAD AND USING A TIMED BASIS

Readings can take as long as or as little time as you choose. You may not be concerned about how long it takes for your own reading. However, it's helpful to set a time frame for your client's reading, especially as you begin to charge money.

Generally speaking, my readings take between one hour to an hour and a half.

Many things hinge on the length of a reading:

- ◆ how in-depth you explain the imagery
- ◆ if you share the history of the Tarot

- the cards' position in the spread
- your client's desire to discuss and ask questions
- what spreads (card laying systems) you choose.

Shorter readings could be emphasized as more of an entertainment style reading. For example, group settings, or if you are hired for a party, restaurant, market, etc.

Great short readings are:

- Three-card spread of Past, Present, Future.
- Five-card spread of Distant Past, Past, Present, Future, Distant Future.
- Diamond spread of four cards, which is useful for more clarity on a client's specific issue.

Larger spreads create longer readings which allow for more freedom to curate what your client needs from their reading.

My "go-to" for a first reading simultaneously facilitates introducing someone to the Tarot and gives them a glimpse of my style of reading cards. It's a four-part reading:

CARD SELECTION AND SPREADS

1. I begin by calculating their numerology and explaining the significance of the life lessons they face in their personal year.

2. I lay a three card reading: past, present, future.

3. I read their Celtic Cross Spread (see Types of Spreads below for an illustration). It's a revelatory perspective of their life and current path.

4. I leave approximately 5-10 minutes for them to ask two or three questions about specific concerns, curiosities, and life's directions.

Since reading cards is a very creative and personalized experience, you may want to find a way to time your client's reading as an aid to stay on track. I normally set a timer to ring ten minutes before the end of the reading to finish off my Celtic Cross spread or primary reading. This allows time for conversation and client questions.

Also, take into consideration that many clients will silently absorb their reading and the information you provide them. They may then wish to reveal the relevancy of the reading to their lives at the end of the session. This can be another layer of catharsis in the reading experience. Be sure to leave time for this aspect towards the end of the session.

It is invaluable for you to learn how and where your intuition was hitting the nail on the head, and how the pieces of the puzzle fit and relate for someone post-read.

If there were any odd or indecipherable feelings you picked up on in the reading, the post-op allows you clarity in hearing how a card or feeling relates to a particular situation or relationship for the client. Even though this portion of the reading may not feel like you are on the clock, the post-reading can be a huge learning tool to assist you to hone your coaching and intuitive abilities.

There is also the possibility that someone will need time after their reading to reflect and "download" all that you have shared. I offer my clients the opportunity to record the reading via voice or video recorder at the beginning of the reading, as some people will not be able to absorb all of it in the first delivery. Also, it is incredibly intriguing for the clients who listen to their reading six months or a year later to see how the dots connect in new ways for them.

I must remind my clients that my memory is not vast enough to remember all that we discuss and what cards come for them in a reading, particularly as I have repeat clients and even regulars. I joke that it's a good thing my intuition is so attuned to mask for my memory deficiency. It will serve you well not to feel as though you're expected to remember each detail of every reading that you deliver.

TYPES OF SPREADS

Three Card Spread

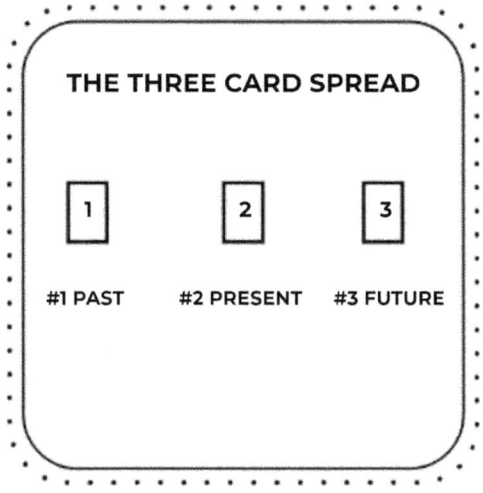

Let's practice reading a Past/Present/Future spread first. Shuffle and choose three cards. The card on your left is the past, in the middle is the present, and to the right is the future.

Let yourself absorb everything your client shares. Maintain eye contact but keep any questions or need for clarification until the end of the reading. It is beneficial after the reading to offer insight on what worked and didn't work during the reading.

Any notes and learnings from this experience:

_____

_____

_____

_____

_____

_____

_____

_____

Five Card Spread

#1 = The Distant Past.
#2 = The Recent Past.
#3 = Present.
#4 = The Near Future.
#5 = The Distant Future.

Diamond Spread

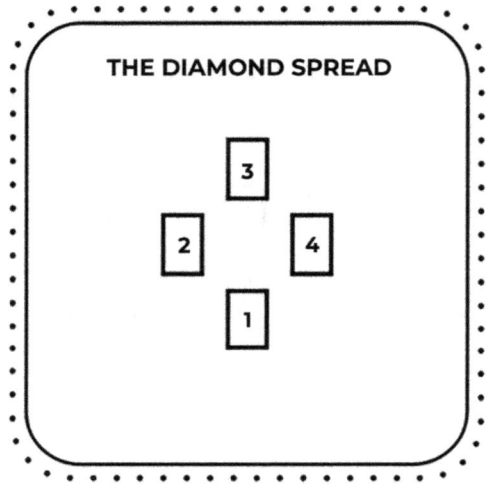

#1 = It deals with this.
#2 = Advisable not to do this.
#3 = You should probably do this.
#4 = This is where it leads or what it's good for.

The Fool's Lifepath Spread

Before shuffling for your client, search the deck for *The Fool* card and lay it aside. Then choose nine cards (face away) and one of you shuffles *The Fool* into those cards making ten. Lay the cards out from left to right.

Reveal all cards and take note of where *The Fool* card is. This represents the person who this reading is for. All cards to the left of *The Fool* represent the past leading up to where *The Fool* is now. All cards to the right of *The Fool* represent where they are headed on their path.

The Relationship Spread

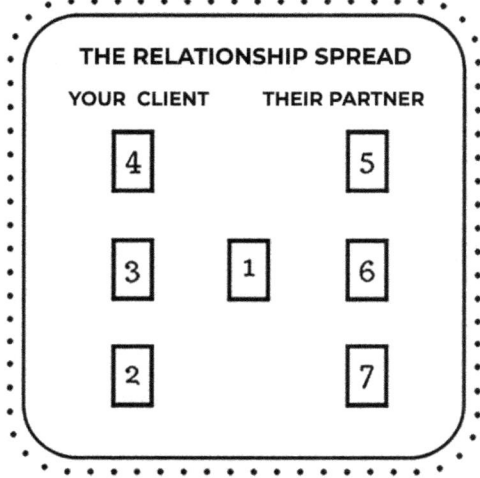

The Left column (three cards down) represents your client on a head, heart, ego level.
Card #4: Your client's head in the relationship.
Card #3: Your client's heart in the relationship.
Card #2: Your client's ego in the relationship.

The Right column (three cards down) represents the partner or person your client is inquiring about.
Card #5: Their head in the relationship.
Card #6: Their heart in the relationship.
Card #7: Their ego in the relationship.

CARD SELECTION AND SPREADS

The card in the middle, #1 represents the theme or lesson of the relationship. It is a great place to start the reading.

You may choose to read the cards in succession from #1 through #7 or across from one another, so you are reading:

> #4 with #5;
> your client's head to their partner's head level.
>
> Then #3 with #6:
> your client's heart in contrast with their partner's heart card.
>
> Then #2 with #7:
> your client's ego in contrast to their partner's ego in the relationship.

The Celtic Cross Spread

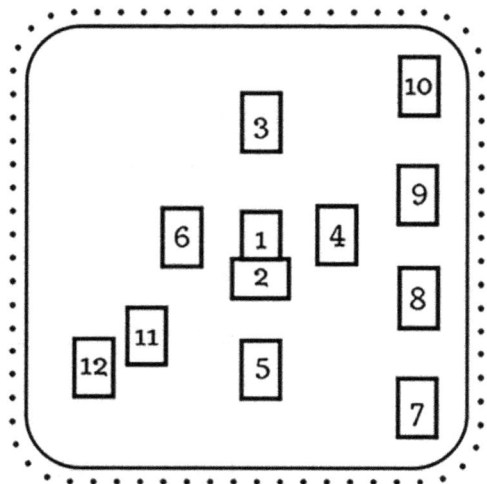

Sarah's Celtic Cross Spread Positions

#1   Present Circumstance + #2 Crossing/Challenge
#3   Destiny/Life Lesson
#4   Distant Past
#5   Recent Past
#6   Future Influences
#7   Further Description of the Present
#8   Relationships
#9   Hopes/Dreams/Desires/Fears
#10 Final Outcome
#11 Timing Card
#12 Advice of the Tarot

Chapter 10

THE "HOW-TO" STRUCTURE OF A TAROT READING

My main objective as a Tarot reader is to uplift the people who come into contact with me. There have been some damaging stereotypes made of card readers, psychics, gifted healers and feelers in the world. While it isn't our job to correct these stereotypes or feed them energy, just be yourself and keep readings integral and professional.

There is no need to dress differently than you usually would or adorn your home for any reason other than to please yourself. If you're inviting clients to your home, the expectation is for it to be tidy and pleasant smelling. Many people have a sensitivity to heavy perfumes and incense smoke, so ask before lighting an incense stick. Create an inviting environment by setting a tone in the space where you are doing the reading. For example:

- ◆ play soft, melodic music (I love harps or instrumental.)
- ◆ have privacy
- ◆ no smoking or drinking
- ◆ turn off all devices (cellphone, laptop, etc.) or set them to silent mode.

Giving your clients and friends the gift of your undivided attention works as a two-way street. They feel important when you are focused on them, and they see you are present with them. They feel valued and seen, and feel they are receiving value for their dollars spent. You have far more to zero in on as an empath when you are tuned into your client. It's absolutely a win-win scenario.

THE "HOW-TO" STRUCTURE OF A TAROT READING

A checklist for the card reading table:

- ☐ Two glasses of water; one for you and one for your client.

- ☐ Chose the card decks and books you will use.

- ☐ Note paper or loose leaf and a pen in case they decide to jot something down.

- ☐ A box of tissues if things get emotional when you explore the depths of their lives.

- ☐ A method for recording time, such as a stopwatch or alarm pre-set on your phone.

- ☐ A pillow for the back of their chair which you can offer to remove once they sit down.

- ☐ A favourite piece that you love, such as a vase or crystal.

- ☐ Optional: Offering them tea or coffee when they arrive.

GETTING STARTED

It's a good idea to minimize the chatter to only a couple of minutes. No matter how polite the client is, they are excited, anxious, and curious to begin the reading. Start by asking them if they've had a reading before and how that experience was for them. Also, ask them if they wish to record the session.

Give them a brief overview of the reading and any significant details about you as a reader:

- ◆ I have been called a clairsentient by many and an old soul.
- ◆ I have been reading cards for nearly 20 years.
- ◆ I specialize in work with the angelic realm and those who have passed over.

This is an excellent place for the story you worked on at the onset of the book. Your clients are naturally curious about you and how you became a reader.

Remember, you are not being asked to qualify yourself or prove your validity as a reader. It may serve you to note your inner dialogue around this topic.

THE "HOW-TO" STRUCTURE OF A TAROT READING

Questions to ask yourself if you feel you want to qualify yourself:

Are you oversharing your spiritual resume to impress your client or validate your credentials as a reader?

Are any of your insecurities coming through or are your nerves related to meeting this person and desiring the best possible reading for them?

Let what you share in the reading with your client do this legwork for you. It is not your job to make someone believe in Tarot cards. A simple "let's consult the cards and see what happens in the reading" will suffice. Share that a Tarot reading is meant to be fun and entertaining, although it often becomes an opportunity to provide coaching and illumination for them.

Ask what brought them in for a reading.

Listen carefully and make notes, especially for new Tarot readers. Asking this question is a matter of self-trust, and as you develop your skills as a reader, it will not feel so vital to your reading.

Share the structure of the Tarot reading.

Let them know what spreads, numerology, and healing work will be involved.

Begin by choosing the shuffling method and laying the cards face down in their spread of choice. Start to notice colour themes and repetitions, followed by recurring shapes and symbols. Identify them to your client and personalize them to their reading's message, highlight, and theme.

The two biggest things your client seeks from you are:

1. Reassurance they are on the right path.

2. Your assistance to reveal to them why they could be in love with their life and themselves.

You accomplish this by bringing their attention to their gifts, character, talents, kindnesses and any other beautiful tidbits that emerge in the cards. Your language, sincerity and intuitive heart will pave the way for that message to be expressed to your client.

Universally, humans need comfort and kindness, and not everyone receives this treatment in everyday life.

THE "HOW-TO" STRUCTURE OF A TAROT READING

You can choose to be a beacon of light for them.

Take caution when "darker" cards emerge (Death, Ten of Swords, Tower, Devil). It serves no one to fear-monger and predict frightening future events to people. Life is challenging enough without another dollop of terror from a Tarot reader to exacerbate life's stressors. As a lightworker, discuss the silver lining in the cards, offer solutions and problem-solve with your client.

Your wisdom, life experience and empathy are your greatest allies. It helps to build a warm, safe tone between you and your client, not unlike a counsellor and their patient. The trust created helps to further dissolve the veil of stereotypical card readers who hold crystal balls and wear gypsy clothing. Even if you only spend that one reading together, the radiance of your spirit in their memory will mean so much more than anything the cards said.

When the reading is finished, offer your contact information to them for questions or checking in. If it feels right, you could ask if it's okay to hug them on their way out. You may choose to create an after reading ritual for yourself for grounding and to re-enter into real-life. At the very least, close your eyes and take three to five long, slow deep breaths. Send wishes to your client for love, health and wellness along their journey. Remember, you are human. No reading is perfect, and once you give the gift of a reading, trust that you will never know all the ways in which it shaped and helped (or will help) your clients. It is the ultimate practice to "*Let Go and Let God*" as often quoted by Dr. Wayne Dyer.

Let's summarize the structure of a reading:

1. *Ask if they have had a reading before.*

2. *Offer them the opportunity to record the reading via voice or video recorder.*

3. *Give them a brief overview of the reading and any significant details about you as a reader.*

4. *(Optional) Ask what brought them in for a reading.*

5. *Share the structure of the Tarot reading, i.e. what spreads, numerology, and healing work will be involved.*

6. *The two biggest things your client needs from you are: reassurance they are on the right path and assistance to reveal to them why*

they could be in love with their life and themselves.

7. *Choose to be a beacon of light in their life.*

8. *Discuss the silver lining in the cards, which is to problem-solve with your client and help them see solutions.*

9. *Build a warm, safe tone between you and your client.*

10. *Offer your contact information to them for questions or checking in.*

11. *Once they leave, close your eyes and take three to five long, slow deep breaths. Send wishes to your client for love, health and wellness along their journey.*

Chapter 11

THE CARDS IN TAROT SPREAD POSITIONS

As a new reader, this part of reading cards seemed the most intimidating to me.

Not only are you reading the face of the card but giving it another layer of meaning with where it is placed within a spread. Do a few readings for yourself before practicing with another person. This is truly something that will take time, practice, and patience to increase your understanding and comfort level.

Spreads are what roots the cards and give them significance in relation to one another.

Let's practice using the **Celtic Cross Spread** and the card "The Sun," which is generally known for its joy, enthusiasm, well-being, health and radiance.

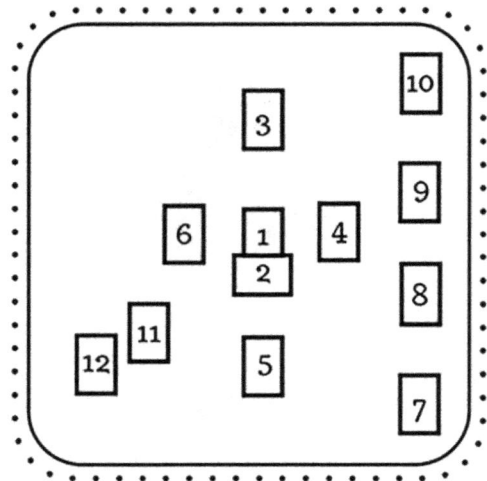

#1 Present Circumstance: You are now experiencing more joy, enthusiasm, well-being, health and radiance.

#2 Crossing/Challenge: You are finding it challenging to attract joy, enthusiasm, well-being, health and radiance.

#3 Destiny/Life Lesson: The reason why your life path is here now is to learn more about joy, enthusiasm, well-being, health and radiance.

THE CARDS IN TAROT SPREAD POSITIONS

#4 Distant Past: In your childhood or younger years, you experienced joy, enthusiasm, well-being, health and radiance.

#5 Recent Past: Recently, there seems to be more joy, enthusiasm, well-being, health and radiance in your life situation.

#6 Future Influences: You can feel joy, enthusiasm, well-being, health and radiance on the horizon.

#7 Further Description of the Present: Joy, enthusiasm, well-being, health and radiance are so important to you now.

#8 Relationships: Your close relationships are joyful, enthusiastic, and feel good. They increase your health and add to your radiance.

#9 Hopes, Dreams, Desires, Fears: Your relationship to joy, enthusiasm, well-being, health and radiance can be complex. It is what you simultaneously yearn for and fear.

#10 Final Outcome: Everything in your life right now is leading you towards an outcome of joy, enthusiasm, well-being, health and radiance.

#11 Timing Card: Now. (We cover timing cards in-depth in READING THE TIMING OF CARDS.)

#12 Advice of the Tarot: The Tarot is advising you to allow your joy, enthusiasm, well-being, health and radiance to continue to be the focal point in your life.

Most spreads have a central theme card; otherwise known as the basis card for the reading. The **Celtic Cross Spread** has its central theme of the reading around card #1. Every other card is connected back to it. It is not necessary to be repetitive in this regard, just knowing that the first card is your theme, assists you to read all the other cards. This is much easier to exhibit with practice.

A demonstration of the thematic relationship to card #1 using a Celtic Cross Spread:

#1 Present Circumstance: Ace of Swords
You are now experiencing a fresh start in how you think and push through old patterns to seek your truth. Your mind is lit up with all the possibilities now.

#2 Crossing/Challenge: XVII The Star
You are finding it challenging to stay in a state of enlightenment. When you recognize yourself as drops of water that form part of the whole lake, you may

remain awakened. (*Tied back to the theme of Ace of Swords:* Allow your new thought patterns to help you stay in connection with your spiritual self and lessons.)

#3 Destiny/Life Lesson: 3 of Swords
You're on this life path to learn how to overcome heartbreak and to cope with loss. (*Tied back to the theme of Ace of Swords*: Your new thinking will help to bring about new coping skills and new awareness to aid the renewal of your heart centre.)

#4 Distant Past: XIII Death
You experienced a profound transformation in your childhood or younger years. Its resulting personal identity re-invention was an incredibly pivotal time for you. *New thought patterns are a part of this process for you now as well.*

#5 Recent Past: 6 of Disks
Recently, there seems to be more optimism towards life and abundance by creating more material security. *It's indicative of the power of your thoughts to shape and influence the world around you.*

#6 Future Influences: 10 of Swords
You can sense there are more challenges to face. These future experiences will complete this cycle of

learning and growing. *Seeing this as an opportunity to practice your new thought patterns, self-talk, perception of life and inner relationship with the Creator will be immensely valuable to overcome these adversities.*

#7 Further Description of the Present: X1 Justice
Harmony, balance and justice are so important to you now, *because you're craving a change in the way you communicate with the world around you and vice versa.*

#8 Relationships: 2 of Disks
Your closest relationship is undergoing a shift *as a result of your new patterns of thought.*

#9 Hopes, Dreams, Desires, Fears: X1X The Sun
Your relationship to joy, enthusiasm, well-being, health and radiance can be complex. It is what you simultaneously yearn for and fear. *You may fear that you will slip into old patterns of thought and communication in your life.*

#10 Final Outcome: Ace of Disks
Everything in your life right now is leading you towards a fresh new financial start, whether it's a complete career change, new business or new income stream. *You have changed and, therefore, your life*

is beginning to reflect the inner changes that you have undergone.

#11 Timing Card: Queen of Cups
Undetermined; up to you. (Translation: there is no pre-set timing for this set of life lessons for you.)

#12 Advice of the Tarot: 8 of Swords
The Tarot is advising you to allow any changes in direction on your path with as much optimism and understanding as you can muster. Allow all things new and shiny to be the focal point in your life.

A reading can be as brief or as expansive as you decide you would like it to be. I will often write out my personal readings in a journal with the brevity that I shared here. I'll go much more in-depth during a paid hour reading by exploring the symbols on the cards, history of the card, colour, and connection to other cards. (For example, if you see multiple 2's or cups in a spread.)

Another idea is to do a "double helix" reading where you lay out two different decks of cards in the same spread. This allows you to have two different points of view from the Tarot in the same card positions within the spread and can be very interesting for both you and the client.

There are books on Tarot spread options and lots of ideas on the internet. Explore and find the spreads that speak to you!

READING THE TIMING OF CARDS

Another useful interpretation of the Tarot is deciphering the timing for a reading. There can be a time value associated with each card should you choose to read them that way. In the Celtic Cross spread, position eleven is the "Timing Card." This card indicates how much time will pass in days, weeks or months until all the concepts and themes are explored. This could be applied to any position, reading or question as you intuit. I am careful not to overly use this timing reading option as it's a very black or white approach to card reading. In general, I like to leave the Tarot to be a highly interpretive tool.

Timing Values for the Cards

Major Arcana
Now; in the present

Minor Arcana
Ace through Ten: one through ten
Page: eleven
Knight: twelve
Cups: days
Rods: weeks
Pentacles: months
Swords, Queens, Kings: Undetermined. Your choice.

Examples:
Nine of Cups: nine days.
Two of Pentacles: two months
Seven of Swords: Undetermined. Your choice.

Chapter 12

TAROT FOR ANSWERING YOUR CLIENT'S LIFE QUESTIONS

A welcome addition is inviting your client to ask questions of the Tarot deck as a "wrap-up" to the reading. I frequently do this to complete a reading. It offers the client a chance to ask about anything that was not addressed in the spreads or numerology that you explored. Or, to ask a specific question, such as, *What sort of partner should I keep an eye out for? Should I stay with my current company or go back to school?*

Open-ended questions about your client's life, family, future, career and money, etc. are all fodder, so this must be blended carefully with the card face and your intuition.

Ways to ask life questions during the wrap up:

1. Have the client touch or shuffle the cards after asking the question, and you will read the top card on the deck.

2. While the client phrases their question about their life, you shuffle the deck. You then place the card deck in front of your client and ask them to cut the deck into two piles. Where they cut the deck becomes the card you read as "their insights into the question" and the one they set aside becomes "the Tarot's answer to their question."

   It is insightful to see how well the two cards relate to one another and adds two perspectives to the answer rather than a singular one.

Answering questions with the Tarot requires you to trust in your ability to connect the dots and relate what the energies, lessons and insights of the cards are to the question presented. It takes practice to decipher between what you feel intuitively versus just relating to your client through your personal story or history.

Sometimes, there are situations that you could not

even fathom that your client is going through or experiencing. You can't know how every situation feels. It's okay to say things like "this isn't something I am familiar with" or "I am not getting a clear sense of how this card relates to your question."

Deliver as much information about the card as you can. It is not your job as a reader to question the material you discuss, but allow it to flow through you as artists and musicians do. Release the need to understand the answer for yourself, and deliver whatever messages you are receiving intuitively along with the metaphor, story, colour, and theme of the card. You can trust that the most meaningful question and answer readings will channel through you as a reader.

I did not offer this aspect of reading cards until I had been reading cards for fifteen years. But, that is not to say that it cannot become part of your readings from the get-go. A great place to start would be to offer to do some readings of question and answer with acquaintances and get their constructive insight. Make sure they ask you questions that you would have no idea what the answer would be to keep the slate clean for yourself. Ultimately, your readings, how and what you offer within them, is entirely your choice. This is just another aspect to keep your readings fresh.

Words to Uplift You!

Being a reader, empath, feeler, seer, psychic does not require you to be or have a perfect life. In fact, it is everything you have strived to become in your life:

- your challenges
- your wisdom
- your perseverance through strife and tragedy
- and overcoming your obstacles learned from hardships endured that are the greatest allies in your readings.

Your ability to relate to your clients creates the most profound readings, not your perfect life or being totally together.

Being spiritual is:

- being real
- being honest
- being vulnerable enough to share from your heart.

This is the gift that you and I are called to share in our perfectly imperfect way. Honour yourself and the Universe by sharing your unique messages with your clients who are fortunate enough to have you read for them. Your grace and greatness already reside there. Tap into your inner sage and enjoy this miraculous ride of channelling readings!

Everything you have gone through, every bit of the despair has been necessary to forge you into a healer and a guide. The need is great. The time is coming soon.

—Ken Jordan of *Reality Sandwich*

APPENDIX A: COLOUR SYMBOLISM

Pink: Softness, femininity, health, beauty, ease

Red: Passion, creativity, conflict, anger/rage, new beginnings, starting over

Orange: (Bright) joy, contentment
(Dull) frustration, stagnancy, anxiety

Yellow: Optimism, happiness, ease, positive flow, illness

Green: Growth, peace, harmony, envy, jealousy, healing

Blue: Emotionality, sensitivity, flow, intuition, sadness, depression

APPENDIX A: COLOUR SYMBOLISM

Purple: Spirit and spirituality, true love, connection to soul, eccentricity, depth

Brown: Earthy, grounded, ferment, blandness, rooting

Black: The unknown and the mysterious, darkness, evil, pure potentiality

Grey: Sadness, neglect, in-between, blended, nonjudgmental

White: Love, enlightenment, safety, purity, boredom, freedom, nothingness, cleansing

BIBLIOGRAPHY

Wikipedia, The Online Dictionary.

Fenton-Smith, Paul, *The Tarot Revealed,* Australia: Allen & Unwin, 2008.

Battistini, Matilde, Translated by Sartarelli, Stephen, *Symbols and Allegories in Art*, Los Angeles: Getty Publications, 2005.

Lewis, James R., *The Astrology Encyclopedia,* Detroit: Gale Research, 1994.

Bowker, John, *World Religions,* New York: DK Publishing, 1997.

Lau, Theodora, *The Handbook of Chinese Horoscopes*, New York: HarperCollins Publishers, 1979.

Alexander, Jane, *The Smudging and Blessings Book*, New York: Sterling Publishing, 1999.

ABOUT THE AUTHOR

Sarah Hayes is the heart of *A Guide To Intuitive Tarot*, and is the creator and facilitator of Tarot Immersion Retreats. Sarah has led thousands of personal, group and couples Tarot readings and healings over the past 27 years. Her expertise lies in blending traditional Tarot life lessons with contemporary psychology to provide intuitive coaching sessions. Her dharma is to brighten all those seeking her counsel and ignite their inner luminosity.

Her wisdom has been cultivated through her creative writing courses at the University of Victoria and her examination of over fifteen different Tarot and Oracle card decks. Sarah was an attendee of the Okanagan's prolific spiritual guru, Cheryl Forrest's *Spiritual Intensive*, for deepening one's healing and reading capabilities. Sarah has also spent time at the Yasodhara Ashram in Nelson, B.C., and studied meditation and yoga at studios, temples, and monasteries in Bali, Maui, Thailand, and Costa Rica.

www.ingramcontent.com/pod-product-compliance
Lightning Source LLC
Chambersburg PA
CBHW070807100426
42742CB00012B/2284